HISTORY & GEOGRAPHY 508
COLD WAR

CONTENTS

Author: Theresa Buskey, J.D.
Editor: Alan Christopherson, M.S.
Illustrations: Brian Ring

Alpha Omega Publications ®

300 North McKemy Avenue, Chandler, Arizona 85226-2618
© MM by Alpha Omega Publications, Inc.   All rights reserved.
LIFEPAC is a registered trademark of Alpha Omega Publications, Inc.

COLD WAR

The end of the biggest war in the history of the world (World War II) was also the beginning of the most complicated war in American history, the Cold War. The Cold War was a battle of ideas, alliances, and fear between the communist countries of the world, led by the Soviet Union, and the free world, led by the United States.

It was rather like two powerful towns that built forts filled with cannons next door to each other, gathered rifles and soldiers, fired shots once in a while, but never quite decided to attack the other fort. The U.S. and the Soviet Union never actually went to war with each other. However, they helped out in wars fought by their allies, spied on each other, built huge collections of atomic bombs to threaten each other, and encouraged or forced other countries to join their side of the "war."

It was a long, expensive, difficult war. It began in 1945 at the end of World War II. It did not end until 1989, when communism collapsed in Europe. This LIFEPAC® will cover the first part of the Cold War from 1945 until about 1970. It will cover the two major wars that were fought by the U.S. against communism in Korea and Vietnam. It will also discuss the way the Vietnam War and the Civil Rights Movement affected America.

OBJECTIVES

Read these objectives. The objectives tell you what you should be able to do when you have successfully completed this LIFEPAC.

When you have finished this LIFEPAC, you should be able to:

1. Describe how the Cold War began.
2. Describe the events and crises of the Cold War.
3. Describe the anti-communist feelings in America and the actions of Senator Joseph McCarthy.
4. Describe the Korean and Vietnam Wars.
5. Describe the Civil Rights Movement.
6. Describe the protests and rebellions of the 1960s.
7. Name the presidents and describe their activities from 1945 to 1973.

VOCABULARY

Study these new words. Learning the meanings of these words is a good study habit and will improve your understanding of this LIFEPAC.

adviser (ad vī' zer). A person who gives an opinion about what should be done
brutal (brü' tl). Cruel; inhuman
censure (sen' shər). An expression of unfavorable opinion; criticism
character (kar' ik tər). Moral strength
contain (kən tān'). To hold back
controversial (kon' trə vėr' shəl). Open to argument or dispute
equality (i kwol' ə tē). The exact likeness in value or rank
hearing (hir' ing). A chance for both sides to speak about an issue or problem

idealist (ī dē' ləst). A person who wants things to be perfect, to live up to a model of the very best

immoral (i môr' əl). Wrong, not right; wicked

missile (mis' əl). A rocket that carries a bomb (can be atomic) to a target (missiles can be launched from land, air or sea)

rebellious (ri bel' yəs). Defying authority; acting to resist or fight against law or authority (like rules of proper behavior)

sponsor (spon' sər). A person or country responsible for a person, nation, or thing

symbol (sim' bəl). Something that stands for or represents something else

underestimate (un' dər es' tə māt). To assume a person or country will do less than they can or will do

upheaval (əp hē' vəl). A large amount of disorder; great changes

vain (vān). Having too much pride in one's ability or achievements

Note: These words appear in **boldface** print the first time they are used in this LIFEPAC. If you are unsure of the meaning when you are reading, review the definition.

Pronunciation Key: hat, āge, cãre, fär; let, ēqual, tėrm; it, īce; hot, ōpen, ôrder; oil; out; cup, pu̇t, rüle; **ch**ild; long; **th**in; /ŦH/ for **th**en; /zh/ for measure; /ə/ represents /a/ in about, /e/ in taken, /i/ in pencil /o/ in lemon, and /u/ in circus.

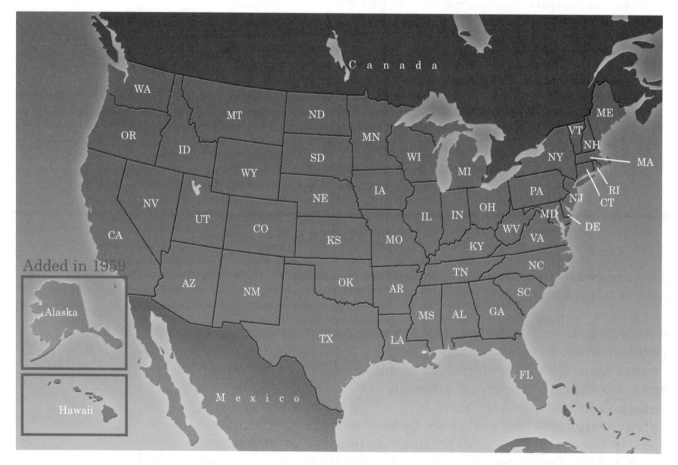

THE UNITED STATES

I. COMMUNIST THREAT

In the course of World War II, the Soviet Union conquered most of eastern Europe. The U.S. expected those nations to be set free to choose their own governments. Instead, they were forced to set up communist governments. The nations of Poland, Czechoslovakia, Hungary, Romania, East Germany, Albania, and Bulgaria became Soviet *satellites*. They were cut off from contact with the free countries and were forced to obey the Soviet Union. Estonia, Latvia, and Lithuania were forced to join the Soviet Union.

At first, the Americans hoped to work with the Soviets, who had been their allies during World War II, but the Soviet dictator, Joseph Stalin, wanted power and he wanted to expand communism. He didn't want to work with the West. America quickly became aware that the Soviets were now a threat to the peace and freedom of the world. Rather than retreat to isolation again, America took the lead to protect the free world. This need to stand against communism was the main cause of the Cold War.

Review these objectives. When you have completed this section, you should be able to:

1. Describe how the Cold War began.
2. Describe the events and crises of the Cold War.
3. Describe the anti-communist feelings in America and the actions of Senator Joseph McCarthy.
7. Name the presidents and describe their activities from 1945 to 1973.

Restudy these words.

brutal	censure	contain
equality	hearing	symbol
underestimate		

Building the Iron Curtain

Communism. To understand the Cold War, it is important to first understand communism. Communism is a form of government in which everything is owned by the government. There is no freedom and the people are controlled by lies. Communism promises people complete **equality**, but in fact, is a very harsh and unfair government.

The government owns all the land, businesses, and factories under communism. Thus, no one can make shoes, cars, baskets, or airplanes unless the government orders them to do it. The government rarely orders the right amount of the things people need, so it is normal not to have enough food or goods under communism.

Also, people are paid for their work by the government and they are not paid more for good work. They also cannot be fired. So, they do as little work as possible, making shoes, cars, and other things that are poor quality and often fall apart. So, people living under communism usually do not have enough of the things they need and what they do have is not very good.

There is no freedom under communism. Usually, one person or a few people run the government. They cannot be voted out of office. When there are elections, the leaders choose who will be elected. Anyone who says that the government is bad or doing something wrong is arrested. Religion is often forbidden and Christians can go to jail or be killed for believing in Jesus.

Communism also works by lying. People are told that their nation is wonderful and that life is awful in the free countries. The people in a communist country are usually not allowed to talk with people from free countries and learn the truth. American newspapers, for example, are forbidden in communist countries because they tell the truth. Communist governments spend a lot of time telling their people how wonderful communism is, no matter how bad things really are.

Lying about everything is a very big part of communism. They even call their nations democracies and republics!! For example, the full name of the Soviet Union was the Union of Soviet Socialist Republics (U.S.S.R.), while East Germany was the German Democratic Republic. Thus, free people have good reasons to be afraid of having their nation conquered by communists.

Post-War Europe. After Germany was defeated in 1945, it was divided into four parts. Each part was run by a different Allied nation: America, Britain, France, and the Soviet Union. The capital, Berlin, was divided up the same way. The Soviets refused to let their part of Germany work with the others. Finally, Britain, France and the U.S. put their three parts together to form the nation of West Germany, a free country. The Soviet Union made their part into a communist country called East Germany.

The Soviet Union also refused to honor its promise to allow free elections in eastern Europe. In the years right after the war, all of the nations taken by the Soviet Union set up communist governments with the help of Soviet soldiers. Yugoslavia created its own communist government and never was fully controlled by the Soviet Union. These new communist countries were not allowed to trade with, work with, or communicate much with the free nations of Europe. Winston Churchill, the former Prime Minister of Great Britain, said that an *Iron Curtain* had

fallen across Europe. It became common during the Cold War to talk about the nations "behind the Iron Curtain."

The Iron Curtain divided Europe into two major alliances. Soon, most of the world was divided also. The free, democratic nations were called Western World or the Free World. The communist countries were called Eastern Bloc or the Communist Bloc. Each side was led by a super power, a large powerful nation that had a huge army and atomic bombs. The Free World was led by the United States and the Communist Bloc was led by the Soviet Union. Some poorer nations were not part of the two sides, they were called the Third World or the Non-Aligned Nations.

Thus, like Europe before World War I, the whole world was divided into two powerful alliances which quickly started an arms race. Except, this time, both sides were building *atomic bombs*. The two sides would, in time, build enough bombs to totally destroy all life on earth if they were all used! The fear that they might start a nuclear (atomic bomb) war is what kept the Cold War from becoming a real war. Both the U.S. and the Soviet Union were too afraid that they and most of the world might be destroyed if a war began.

 Answer these questions.

1.1 What were the nine countries behind the Iron Curtain in Europe?

_____

_____

_____

1.2 Is religion usually allowed in a communist country? _____

1.3 What happened to the part of Germany occupied by the Soviet Union?

_____

_____

1.4 What were the two super powers afraid of if a real war had started between them?

_____

_____

1.5 What were the four nations that occupied Germany in 1945?

_____

_____

1.6 What were the two "super powers" of the Cold War?

_____

1.7   What were the names for the nations that were not communist, led by the U.S.?

_____

1.8   What were the names for the communist nations?

_____

1.9   What were the names for the poorer countries that were not on either side in the

Cold War? _____

_____

 Complete these sentences.

1.10   Communism is a way of government in which _____ is owned
       by the government, there is no _____ , and the people are
       controlled by _____ .

1.11   Winston Churchill said that Europe was divided between communist and free
       countries by an _____ .

1.12   Communism promises people complete _____ .

Division Problem

Containment. The Soviets wanted more communist countries beyond what they already had taken after the war. They tried (but failed) to use their army to get a communist government in Iran, an oil rich nation south of the Soviet Union. They also were helping communist fighters in Greece that were trying to overthrow the government there. All this scared the United States. In 1947, President Truman decided to help the people of Greece fight off the communists. With the support of Congress, money was sent to Greece and Turkey to help the governments there get weapons and supplies. The communists were defeated in both nations.

Truman began the U.S. policy called *Containment.* It would be the U.S. plan for all of the Cold War. Truman knew he could not overthrow communism in the Soviet Union and eastern Europe without starting another world war. So, he decided to **contain** communism, to keep it from spreading. He committed the U.S. to give help to any nation on earth that might be attacked by people trying to set up a communist government. Most of the battles of the Cold War were caused by someone backed by the Soviet Union trying to spread communism to a new country and someone, with American help trying to stop them.

Marshall Plan. All of Europe had been badly damaged by World War II. Homes and factories were destroyed. People were homeless. There were few jobs. The people needed help and they were beginning to listen to the communists. Like the dictators during the Great Depression, the communists were promising to fix things if they were given power in the governments. The U.S. realized that something had to be done to help Europe before the communists took over more countries.

6

The U.S. Secretary of State in 1948 was George Marshall. He had been an important general during the war. He was based in Washington, D.C. and responsible for all of the U.S. military. He came up with a plan to help Europe. It was called the *Marshall Plan.*

The Marshall Plan gave billions of dollars to European countries to help them rebuild. It was an incredible success. Europe rebuilt its factories, restarted its trade, and began to care for its people. All of the nations of western Europe took part in the Marshall Plan. None of those nations became communist. The Communist Bloc countries did not receive help from the Plan, however. The Soviet Union would not allow it.

Berlin Airlift. Berlin, the capital of Germany before the war, was located deep inside the Soviet section of Germany. In 1948 the Soviets decided to force the other Allies to leave the city and give it to them. They did this by blockading the western parts of the city. This meant that the people of Berlin could not get food or supplies because the western nations could not use the roads or trains to ship it across Soviet occupied land.

However, Stalin had **underestimated** President Truman. Truman did not want to fight a war over Berlin, but he was not willing to give up all those people to communism either. He ordered the air force to supply West Berlin by air. It was named the *Berlin Airlift.*

The Berlin Airlift was a huge job. Every single one of the two million people in West Berlin had to get their food, clothes, fuel, and

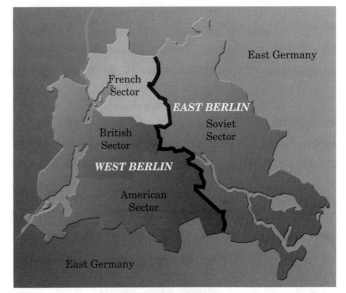

DIVIDED BERLIN

supplies by airplane. The planes landed at the main airport in West Berlin every three minutes around the clock. The German people began to see the Americans as friends after that, not as enemies who had conquered their land.

The Soviets were surprised. They did not expect the Americans to work so hard to help the Germans. They finally gave up and ended the blockade after almost a year. West Berlin would stay a free city in the middle of a communist country until the Cold War ended.

Berlin Wall. The free city of West Berlin would be a major problem for the communist government of East Germany. German refugees who wanted to escape communism could go to Berlin and cross to freedom in the western side of the city. West Germany made these immigrants citizens right away. Many skilled people like doctors, writers, and engineers left this way because the communist government did not allow them freedom or reward them for their work. Thousands of East Germany's smartest and most capable people fled this way in the years after the war.

Finally, the government of East Germany had enough. In 1961, they built a wall around West Berlin to keep the people of East Germany from leaving. It was called the Berlin Wall and it was the most important **symbol** of the Cold War.

BERLIN AIRLIFT

The Berlin Wall was a huge cement wall with barbed wire or round tubes at the top that kept people from climbing over it. Behind the wall was a wide strip of empty land patrolled by soldiers and guard dogs. Many people were shot and killed trying to cross the wall between 1961 and 1989. Some also succeeded and made it to freedom by running and climbing, crashing through the wall with trucks, tunneling under the wall, or going over it on wires.

Soviet Control. The Soviet Union forced the nations of the Communist Bloc to stay communist all the way through the Cold War. Hungary, for example, tried to end communism in their country in 1956. They revolted against the Hungarian communist dictators and set up a new government. The Soviet Union immediately invaded, killing thousands of people who supported the revolt. Many more thousands left the country to live in the west.

Czechoslovakia also tried to change communism in their country in 1968. A new Czech leader tried to give the people more freedom and let them have some control over the government. The other nations of the Communist Bloc invaded in 1969 to stop the reforms. Again the leaders were killed and communist dictators were put back in power.

As late as 1980, the people of Poland protested for better pay and reforms. They created a free union, that was not controlled by the government, called Solidarity. The Polish government was forced to accept Solidarity and began some reforms. However, when it looked like the Soviet Union might invade, the Polish army took over the government. They imprisoned or killed the leaders of Solidarity and restored communist rules for the land. Thus, for all of the Cold War, eastern Europe was forced to remain communist by the Soviet Union. The use of force also made many Americans understand just how **brutal** and dangerous communism was.

THE BERLIN WALL

NATO. As the Soviet Union took over eastern Europe and threatened southern Europe, America and the nations of the west became very concerned. They were afraid that the U.S.S.R. might start conquering the nations of newly freed western Europe also. To prevent this, the free democracies decided to form a permanent alliance. The U.S. had not signed an alliance since the Revolutionary War, but it signed this one.

The North Atlantic Treaty Organization (NATO) was formed in 1949. It included the United States, Canada, Great Britain, France, and other European nations. Eventually, West Germany would also join. The treaty behind NATO stated that any attack on one member was considered an attack on all of the members. Thus, the NATO allies agreed to stand together to fight the Soviets if they ever did invade western Europe.

The Soviet Union was not pleased with the new alliance. They accused the west of trying to start another war. They also made their satellites in eastern Europe sign their own alliance, called the Warsaw Pact. It was not necessary because obviously the communist nations would fight if the Soviet Union told them to do it. The Warsaw Pact dissolved at the end of the Cold War, but NATO continues to exist.

Name the item, person or event.

1.13 _____ West Berlin got all of its supplies by air in 1948-49

1.14 _____ The U.S. policy toward communism during the Cold War

1.15 _____ Gave money to Europe to rebuild after World War II

1.16 _____ Way that East Germany stopped its people from fleeing to the west through Berlin, important Cold War symbol

1.17 _____ U.S. Secretary of State, general in charge of all of the U.S. military in World War II

1.18 _____ President who decided to stop communism from spreading

1.19 _____ Two Communist Bloc nations that were invaded to save

_____ communism there.

1.20 _____ Polish free union of the 1980s

1.21 _____ Permanent alliance to protect western Europe

1.22 _____ Communist, Cold War alliance in eastern Europe

 Answer these questions.

1.23 What caused most of the battles of the Cold War?

_____

_____

1.24 Why didn't the eastern European countries join the Marshall Plan?

_____

1.25 What were the first two nations America sent money to help stop communism?

_____

1.26 What kind of people were leaving East Germany before 1961?

_____

1.27 What is the full name of NATO?

_____

China and Taiwan

CHIANG KAI-SHEK

Chiang Kai-shek. China had been ruled by emperors until the early part of the 20th century. The last emperor gave up his throne in 1912 to a group that was trying to set up a republic. But, there was a lot of fighting and it was not until 1928 that a government under Chiang Kai-shek, the head of the Nationalist Party, was able to control the huge country. However, shortly after that, Japan invaded and occupied parts of China. Chiang was recognized as the leader of free China and was a U.S. ally during World War II.

There was also a group of communists who wanted to rule in China. They were led by a very clever man named Mao Zedong. When the Japanese invaded, the Communists and the Nationalists agreed to work together to fight them. That lasted until near the end of the war; when it became clear that Japan was going to be defeated by the Allies, Mao and Chiang began fighting each other again.

The Soviet Union declared war on Japan just days before it surrendered. They invaded Northern China, capturing a large part of the land there. They gave this land with all its industries and supplies to Mao and the communists. Mao became more and more powerful. The U.S. did not want to get involved in a Chinese civil war and did not give Chiang all the help they could. Also, Mao was better organized and a better fighter. In 1949, Chiang fled to the island of Taiwan and set up a government there. Taiwan is still independent from China to this day.

Communist China. Many people in America were shocked that the U.S. had "lost" China to communism. However, it was not clear that America could have stopped it without getting into another long, hard war in a foreign land. For many years, however, the U.S. would not recognize Communist or Red China. The U.S. said that the government of Taiwan (Nationalist China) was the real government of China. Taiwan even held the seat kept for China in the United Nations until 1971.

Mao Zedong was a communist who really believed he could make everyone equal and solve all of his nations problems using communist ideas. He killed many of the powerful landowners in China and gave their land to the poor farmers (peasants). He cut his nation off completely from the free world to protect his pure communism.

Then, he started the "Great Leap Forward" in 1958. This was supposed to make China into a great industrial country in just a few years. Land was taken away from the peasants and put together in large farms called communes. The farmers who used to own the land were forced to work on the communes for wages. The wages did not go up if the work was done well or the harvest was big. People were forced to work extra hours, machines were used around the

MAO ZEDONG

clock without even stopping to take care of problems. Many people starved and business was ruined.

Many of the leaders in China realized that the strict controls of communism were hurting the production of food and goods. They wanted to try things that were not so strongly communist. Mao hated that idea. In 1966, he started the Cultural Revolution to force the nation to use only communist ideas and kill anyone who did not agree. Mao sent gangs of young people to attack centers of power and learning. Universities were closed and many local governments were taken over by the gangs, called Red Guards. Finally, even Mao realized the Red Guards were too wild and had the army stop them. Again the businesses of the nation were damaged and many people died.

The U.S.S.R. and China did not agree on how a communist nation should act. Mao believed that communist and capitalist (free) nations would have to go to war for control of the world. The Soviet Union, fearing a nuclear war, was not willing to do this, especially after Joseph Stalin died in 1953; so the two nations stopped helping each other by 1960 and even fought some battles with each other along their border. However, the U.S. did not realize for many years that these two nations were actually enemies. Americans thought all communist nations would work together to try and make the whole world communist. Thus, the U.S. treated both nations as Cold War enemies.

 **Complete these sentences.**

1.28 The war time leader of China who was an American ally was

_____ .

1.29 In the Chinese civil war, _____ led the Communists

and _____ led the Nationalists.

1.30 The _____ in 1958 was an attempt to make China an industrial power in a few years.

1.31 For many years, the U.S. government said that the real government of China was the government on the island of _____ .

1.32 The _____ was Mao's attempt in 1966 to use the Red Guards to force China to use only strict communist ideas.

1.33 After 1960, the Soviet Union and China were really _____ even though both were communist.

Anti-Communism in America

Post-War America. Americans after World War II knew they could not go back to isolation like after World War I. The danger from communism was just too great. At first, America tried to bring all their soldiers home, but the threats in Europe remained too great. Americans accepted by 1949 that they would have to keep the army and navy ready to fight at all times. Unlike past wars the military was not dramatically cut back. American soldiers were kept in Europe, Japan, and other parts of the world to be ready to fight if the communists did.

Most of the soldiers, however, did come home and quickly found jobs. The Great Depression was still on everyone's mind, but it did not come back after the war. People had earned lots of money working during the war, but they could not buy much because most of the factories were making things for the war. So, after the war Americans used the money they had saved to buy cars, refrigerators, new clothes, toys, shoes, radios, record players, and all sorts of things. The factories could not produce the goods fast enough. There were plenty of jobs for Americans.

Harry S. Truman had become president when Franklin D. Roosevelt died in 1945. He was elected president in 1948. He put together his own program to add to the New Deal. He called it the Fair Deal. He wanted laws to protect employees from discrimination and more New Deal type programs, like a national program to pay for doctor bills and higher wages. The Republican Congress would not cooperate, however, and very little of the Fair Deal ever became law.

Ike. Dwight D. Eisenhower (whose nickname was Ike) had been the Allied commander in Europe. He was very popular in the United States. He ran for president in 1952, winning easily. He had one of the most famous campaign slogans in American history, "I like Ike."

After he won, he did not undo all the New Deal laws, as many Republicans hoped he would. The New Deal programs like minimum wage (a law setting the lowest amount a person can be paid) and Social Security (a plan to pay money to people when they are too old to work) became a permanent part of American life. Future presidents would add to them or change them but never get rid of them. Thus, the idea that the government had to use its money to help people and businesses continued after the Depression was over.

The Soviet Union built its own atomic bomb in 1949, stealing some of the information from the U.S. This started the nuclear arms race that lasted through most of the Cold War. In 1957 the Soviets beat the U.S. by launching the first man-made satellite, called Sputnik. This started a space race between the two super powers.

The space race was a contest between the U.S and the Soviet Union to build satellites and ships to explore space. The two sides competed hard in this race. Each side was afraid of having the other develop important new kinds of rockets and controls that might be used against the other.

The Soviet Union put the first man in

NEIL ARMSTRONG, THE FIRST MAN ON THE MOON

JULIUS AND ETHEL ROSENBERG

orbit in 1961. They also set many records for the longest time in space in their space station named *Mir* in the 1980s and '90s. However, the United States space organization, NASA (National Aeronautics and Space Administration), set its own records. America would put the first man on the moon in 1969. America also built the first reusable space ship, the Space Shuttle, which began flights in 1981. The things that were learned from the space race would improve or create many kinds of goods like computers, rockets, fabrics, smoke detectors, and insulation.

Fear. Many people in the United States were very afraid of communism. They saw the people of eastern Europe and China loose their freedom. They heard about all the people who were killed for disobeying communist governments. Also, communists claimed that they would soon take over the world.

Communist parties were working all over the world to set up new communist governments, even in the United States. Many of these communist groups got money and help from the Soviet Union. A few of these communists also became spies for the Soviets. Americans were very afraid of having communist spies helping the Soviet Union destroy our freedoms.

In 1948 an important man in the State Department (which controls relations with other countries) was accused of being a communist spy. The man's name was Alger Hiss. The man who accused him was an American who had worked for the Soviets, but changed sides. He presented enough proof for Hiss to be convicted of lying when he said he wasn't a spy.

In 1951, a husband and wife named Julius and Ethel Rosenberg were convicted of spying for the Soviets. They had given some of America's secrets on how to build an atomic bomb to the communists. They were executed in 1953.

JOSEPH MCCARTHY

McCarthyism. These two events scared Americans even more. Americans were so frightened that they listened to Senator Joseph McCarthy who, in the early 1950s, made accusations about there being communist spies all through the government of the U.S. McCarthy was never able to prove his accusations, but, at first, it did not matter. People were so scared they believed him just for saying it!

McCarthy used fear to investigate people all over the U.S. People he accused had to prove they weren't communists. Many people who were interested in communist ideas, but would never betray their country, were forced to leave their jobs. Other people who could not or would not answer McCarthy's accusations also left their jobs in fear. People all over the country were "black-balled," forbidden to work at their jobs because someone had accused them of being a communist. The fear and unfairness of this hunt for spies was given the name "McCarthyism." It is used for any large hunt for wrong doing that is unfair and based on fear.

In the early 1950s television was just becoming popular. In 1954, **hearings** in the Senate about McCarthy's accusations were shown to the whole nation on TV. People saw him make all kinds of unproven statements about communists in the army. He looked and acted like a bully. The public hearing made many people start distrusting McCarthy. His hunt for communists was stopped and he was **censured** by the Senate. Some people believe that his unfair ways kept America from making a careful, fair search for the *real* communist spies that were working in our country.

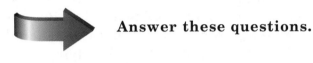 **Answer these questions.**

1.34 What is McCarthyism? _____

_____

1.35 Why didn't the Great Depression come back after World War II?

_____

_____

1.36 What was Harry S. Truman's program to add to the New Deal called?

_____

1.37 What was Dwight D. Eisenhower's campaign slogan?

_____

1.38 Who was Alger Hiss? _____

_____

1.39 Who were the Rosenbergs? _____

_____

1.40 How did McCarthy get so much attention? _____

_____

1.41 What finally made people stop trusting Joseph McCarthy?

_____

1.42 What is the U.S. space organization?

_____

1.43 What was the first man-made satellite and who launched it?

_____

1.44 What nation put the first man on the moon? When?

_____

1.45 What nation put the first man in orbit? When?

_____

1.46 How did the Senate treat McCarthy after his communist hunt was stopped?

_____

 Review the material in this section in preparation for the Self Test. The Self Test will check your mastery of this particular section. The items missed on this Self Test will indicate specific areas where restudy is needed for mastery.

SELF TEST 1

Match these people (each answer, 2 points).

1.01 _____ Senator who made accusations about communists in America

1.02 _____ Communist Chinese leader

1.03 _____ State Department man accused of being a communist spy

1.04 _____ Executed for giving American atomic secrets to the Soviets

1.05 _____ American general at home in World War II, Secretary of State after the war

1.06 _____ Nationalist Chinese leader

1.07 _____ Communist dictator of the Soviet Union

1.08 _____ Campaign slogan, "I like Ike"

1.09 _____ President at the end of World War II, set up U.S. policy to deal with communism during the Cold War

a. Joseph Stalin

b. Harry S. Truman

c. Dwight D. Eisenhower

d. George Marshall

e. Chiang Kai-shek

f. Mao Zedong

g. Joseph McCarthy

h. Alger Hiss

i. Julius & Ethel Rosenberg

Answer these question. (each answer, 4 points).

1.010 What is communism? _____

_____

_____

1.011 What happened to the nations of eastern Europe after World War II?

_____

_____

1.012 What was the American policy of Containment during the Cold War?

_____

_____

1.013 Who were the leaders of the two sides during the Cold War and what were the

names of the sides? _____

_____

_____

1.014 Why did the Great Depression not return after World War II?

_____

_____

1.015 Why was there so much fear of communism in America in 1950?

_____

_____

1.016 Why were things like shoes and cars made poorly in communist countries?

_____

_____

1.017 What was the most important reason why the U.S. and the Soviet Union did not

go to war with each other during the Cold War? _____

_____

1.018 How were Germany and Berlin divided after World War II?

_____

_____

1.019 What was Mao Zedong trying to do in the Great Leap Forward in 1958?

_____

_____

Name the item, person, or thing (each answer, 3 points).

1.020 _____ Wall built to keep East Germans from escaping to the west through the capital city

1.021 _____ Island that was considered the real government of China by the U.S. in the 1950s and '60s

1.022 _____ U.S. program that gave Europe money to rebuild after World War II

1.023 _____ How Berlin was kept supplied when the Soviets blockaded the city in 1948

1.024 _____ Polish free union in the 1980s

1.025 _____ Treaty organization the U.S. joined to protect western Europe from the Soviet Union

1.026 _____ First man-made satellite, 1957

1.027 _____ American space agency

1.028 _____ Name for the dividing line between free and communist Europe, came from Winston Churchill

1.029 _____ The communist treaty organization that was supposed to protect eastern Europe

Write *true* **or** *false* **on the blank** (each answer, 2 points).

1.030 _____ America returned to isolation after World War II.

1.031 _____ People in communist countries are not allowed to talk freely with people in free countries.

1.032 _____ Communists often call their countries republics or democracies.

1.033 _____ Czechoslovakia was a faithful communist nation all through the Cold War.

1.034 _____ Dwight D. Eisenhower ended many of the New Deal programs and went back to how the government was run before the Great Depression.

1.035 _____ The Soviets built the first reusable space craft, the Space Shuttle.

Score
Adult Check

_____
Initial   Date

II. HOT WAR AND CRISES

The Cold War was called cold because the Soviet Union and the U.S. did not ever go to war with each other. That would be called a hot war. But, there were several hot wars fought between communists and the U.S. or its allies from 1945 to 1989. Two of these were major wars in Korea and Vietnam. The U.S. sent a large army to fight in both of those wars.

Besides the real, hot wars, there were many crises during the Cold War. These were times when something brought the two sides close to war or made them so angry with each other that peace was difficult to maintain. Several of these, as well as the Korean and Vietnam Wars, will be covered in this section.

Review these objectives. When you have completed this section, you should be able to:

2. Describe the events and crises of the Cold War.
4. Describe the Korean and Vietnam Wars.
7. Name the presidents and describe their activities from 1945 to 1973.

Restudy these words.

adviser	controversial	missile
sponsor	vain	

Korean War

Divided Korea. When the Soviet Union invaded northern China at the end of World War II, it also captured the northern part of the country of Korea. As in Europe, the Soviet Union refused to allow the two parts of Korea to work together and elect a free government. Instead, the Soviets set up a communist government in North Korea. This new government had a large army that had many good weapons that the Soviets had given them.

The Americans had set up a free government in South Korea after the war. By 1950, the U.S. had taken all of its army out of Korea and left the country to be run by its own people. North Korea decided it would be a good time to conquer the whole country for communism. Joseph Stalin probably approved of the plan. He thought

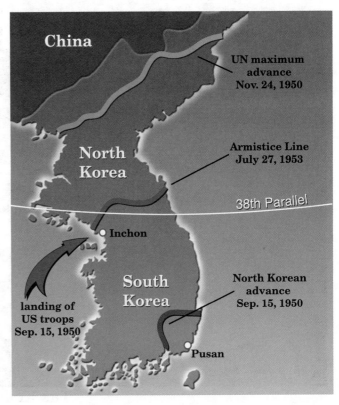

China

North Korea

South Korea

UN maximum advance Nov. 24, 1950

Armistice Line July 27, 1953

38th Parallel

Inchon

North Korean advance Sep. 15, 1950

landing of US troops Sep. 15, 1950

Pusan

the North Koreans would win quickly and the U.S. would be unable to do anything about it.

United Nations. North Korea invaded the South in June of 1950, crossing the 38th parallel, the map line that was the border. However, President Truman was not about to let this happen. He remembered the appeasement of dictators in the 1920s and 30s. He did not want to sit back and let the communists grab countries one by one as Hitler had done.

Truman asked the United Nations to act. The Soviet Union was not there because they were angry about Taiwan holding China's U.N. seat. Therefore, the Soviets could not stop the U.N. from acting. The U.N. voted that North Korea was being an aggressor and called for soldiers to help South Korea. Truman sent the American army right away.

Thus, the Korean War was officially fought by a United Nations army. Sixteen nations would send soldiers to fight there, but the biggest army came from the United States. The U.N. commander was an American general, Douglas MacArthur, who had recaptured New Guinea and the Philippines during World War II.

MacArthur had a very big problem at the beginning of the war. The North Korean army had captured almost all of South Korea. The U.N. and South Korean army were holding only a small piece of land around the city of Pusan. This line held by the U.N. and South Korean soldiers was called the *Pusan Perimeter*. It would be very hard for MacArthur to break through the Perimeter and fight his way back up the Korean peninsula.

However, MacArthur had a better idea for a different kind of attack. He remembered the amphibious attacks he had made along the coast of New Guinea, attacking from the sea. He did the same thing again in September of 1950. He landed his men at Inchon <u>behind</u> where the North Koreans were fighting. The landing was a huge success. The northern army could not fight both in front and behind. They began to retreat. By November of 1950, the U.N. army had pushed way into North Korea, almost to the Chinese border.

MacArthur was a very **vain** man. He ignored people who tried to warn him that the Chinese would not like the U.N. army

THE KOREAN WAR

HISTORY & GEOGRAPHY

LIFEPAC TEST

Name _____

Date _____

Score _____

Possible Score _____ 100

Name the person, place, event or thing (each answer, 4 points).

1. _____ Government that owns everything, allows no freedom and lies constantly

2. _____ Commander in Korea, fired for publically fighting his orders

3. _____ Wall built to keep East Germans from escaping to the west through Berlin

4. _____ Resolution by Congress that gave President Johnson the power to do whatever was needed to stop Vietnamese communists

5. _____ Chiang Kai-shek was the leader of this Chinese group

6. _____ Fidel Castro became the communist leader of this island nation

7. _____ U.S. program to rebuild Europe after World War II

8. _____ Dividing line between the communist and free nations of Europe during the Cold War

9. _____ Mao Zedong was the leader of this Chinese group

10. _____ The American space agency

Choose the correct letter (each answer, 3 points).

11. _____ was the U.S. president that got America out of the Vietnam War.
   a. John Kennedy   c. Richard Nixon
   b. Dwight Eisenhower   d. Lyndon Johnson

12. The main reason the U.S.S.R. and America did not go to war during the Cold War was _____ .
   a. they were still friendly after being allies in World War II.
   b. the U.S. was isolationist after World War II.
   c. both sides were afraid of a nuclear war
   d. communists did not want war

B

13. The nations of east Europe, taken during World War II by the Soviet Union _____ .

   a. were forced to become and stay communist during the Cold War

   b. were forced to join the Soviet Union

   c. became free countries after the U.S. threatened to start a war for them

   d. were communist for only part of the Cold War

14. In the Cuban Missile Crisis, the Soviet Union tried to _____ .

   a. fire missiles at Cuba

   b. put missiles in Cuba

   c. sell missiles to other countries from Cuba

   d. blockade Cuba with missiles

15. The Korean War was fought between North Korea and _____ .

   a. the United States   c. the Soviet Union

   b. NATO   d. the United Nations

16. _____ was not communist during the Cold War.

   a. Hungary   c. Poland

   b. West Germany   d. China

17. The Civil Rights Movement _____ .

   a. used peaceful protests   c. was led by Rosa Parks

   b. did not succeed   d. fought to continue segregation

18. The most wide-spread protests in the 1960s and '70s were about _____ .

   a. communism   c. pollution

   b. making drugs legal   d. the Vietnam War

19. Vietnam was a difficult war for America because _____ .

   a. we did not win   c. it was our longest war

   b. people hated it   d. all of these

20. Senator Joseph McCarthy became famous by _____ .

   a. fighting against the war in Vietnam

   b. making accusations about communists in the government

   c. organizing the military to fight in Korea and Vietnam

   d. leading the Civil Rights Movement in Congress

C

Answer *true* **or** *false*. **If the answer is false change one or more of the underlined words to make it true** (each answer, 3 points). (Give 1 point for a correct "false" answer when the student cannot make the statement true).

21. _____ *Brown v. Board of Education of Topeka* was a Supreme Court decision that made segregation illegal in schools.

22. _____ The U-2 Incident was about a <u>Soviet</u> spy plane that was shot down.

23. _____ During the Cold War, Vietnam, Korea and <u>France</u> were all divided with one part being communist and the other not for a time.

24. _____ The U.S. policy toward communism during the Cold War was called <u>Confrontation</u>.

25. _____ The Berlin Airlift kept the city supplied when the <u>Germans</u> blockaded the city in 1948.

26. _____ The <u>Soviet Union</u> put the first man-made satellite and person in orbit.

27. _____ The people of the United States were very afraid of <u>communism</u> in the 1950s.

28. _____ <u>Lyndon Johnson</u> and Martin Luther King were both assassinated in the 1960s.

29. _____ <u>The Warsaw Pact</u> was the treaty organization joined by the U.S. to protect Europe from the Soviet Union during the Cold War.

30. _____ In wars all over the world during the Cold War, the U.S. would help one side while <u>East Germany</u> helped the other.

fighting up so close to their land. MacArthur believed the Communist Chinese government would not do anything and even if they did, he could defeat them. However, MacArthur was wrong. The huge Chinese army crossed the border in November to attack the U.N. army, which was not ready for such an attack. The Chinese government said the soldiers were just volunteers who were coming on their own to help their brother communists, but that was just another communist lie. The men who attacked MacArthur were well-trained soldiers commanded by experienced officers who had fought in World War II and the Chinese Civil War.

MacArthur was driven back until he was again inside South Korea. He was humiliated and furious. He wanted the U.S. to attack China. However, Truman and the army commanders in America were afraid of starting World War III. The border of China and Korea was close to the southern border of the Soviet Union, which now had atomic bombs. The American leaders did not want a war in Asia with China and the Soviet Union which might become a nuclear war.

With the threat of nuclear war in mind, the American commanders refused to allow MacArthur to bomb or attack China in any way. They wanted to fight for Korea, but only in Korea. This was called a limited war. A limited war was one in which the two sides fought only in the one place. They did not attack countries that were helping the enemy in the war. It was limited to a certain place, in this case, Korea.

MacArthur thought this was a foolish way to fight a war. He had a point. It was difficult to win a war when another country could send in all the soldiers and supplies it wanted without being attacked. However, MacArthur was an American soldier. It was his job to obey the president, even when he did not like it. When the general began to argue about his orders in public and try to get the American people to side with him, Truman fired him.

The American people were very angry with President Truman for firing Douglas

GENERAL DOUGLAS MACARTHUR

MacArthur. The general was a very popular war hero. However, when he came home, an investigation showed that many of the other American generals, who were also war heroes, agreed with Truman. MacArthur lost much of his support and never held another military command in the U.S.

When the U.N. army had managed to fight its way back to the old border between the two Koreas, Truman asked for peace talks. The North Koreans with their Chinese and Soviet **sponsors**, agreed. The peace could have been made right away except for the problem of prisoners. Many of the North Korean and Chinese prisoners did not want to go back to their communist countries after the war. The communists insisted they had to be sent home, even if they did not want to go. The United Nations refused to force them.

The peace talks got stuck because of this issue. The two sides kept fighting, but nothing changed. Both sides managed to hang on to most of their old land. Finally, in 1953, Joseph Stalin died and the new Soviet leaders agreed to peace without forcing the prisoners to go home. The peninsula was divided again along the 38th parallel and the war ended; however, no peace treaty was ever signed. They just agreed to a "cease fire," to stop fighting. To this day, communist North Korea and free South Korea are still at war with each other and they still shoot at each other occasionally. However, they have kept their agreement not to actually fight the war since 1953.

Complete these sentences.

2.1 The commander of the United Nations army in Korea was

_____ .

2.2 The Korean War began in 1950 when _____

_____ .

2.3 The type of government in North Korea was

_____ .

2.4 The Soviets did not stop the U.N. from acting about Korea because they were absent, upset by the fact that _____

_____ .

2.5 At the beginning of the war, the U.N. army only held a little piece of land behind the

_____ .

2.6 MacArthur was able to take almost all of Korea after a successful landing at

_____ .

2.7 The peace talks got stuck because the communists insisted that all prisoners had to

_____ whether they wanted to

or not.

2.8 When MacArthur publicly fought his orders, Truman

_____ .

2.9 After the war, Korea was divided along the _____ .

2.10 The North Koreans were saved from defeat by

_____ .

2.11 The Korean War was officially fought between North Korea and

_____ .

Crises

Thaws. The death of Stalin in 1953 brought the first of many *thaws* in the Cold War. Thaws often came when the communists decided to negotiate and fix problems rather than threaten and lie. A thaw was usually a time when the two sides were nicer to each other and even managed to work out some of the problems between their counties. The thaws usually ended, however, when a crisis made one or both sides angry or afraid again.

At Stalin's death, the Soviets started the first thaw by agreeing to reunite Austria. It had been divided into four parts and occupied like Germany, but unlike Germany,

22

when the Soviets left in 1955, Austria became a free country.

The new leader of the Soviet Union, Nikita Khrushchev, told the U.S. that he wanted *peaceful coexistence* and that he did not want war. The Americans did not trust the Soviets, but they did start trying to get along with them better. However, this first thaw ended in 1956 when the Soviet army invaded Hungary to stop that country from overthrowing its communist government.

U-2. The United States was very concerned about **missile** bases the U.S.S.R. might be building. In the 1950s, there were no satellites that could take pictures of the earth to spot missile bases or atomic bomb test sites. Instead, the U.S. used special spy planes that flew so high above the Soviet Union that no one knew they were there taking pictures.

In May of 1960, one of these planes, called the U-2, was shot down over Soviet territory. The pilot, Francis Gary Powers, was captured and admitted he was on a spy mission. President Eisenhower admitted he had sent the plane, but he refused to apologize or stop the flights. Khrushchev was very angry. He had visited the U.S. in 1959 during this thaw. However, now he refused to allow President Eisenhower to visit the U.S.S.R., as they had planned.

Cuba. A dictator named Fidel Castro took over the island of Cuba, just south of Florida, in 1959. He took away all of the American land and businesses in Cuba for the government. He also announced he was a communist. The American leaders were very nervous about having a communist country so close to the United States. They were also angry about all of the American property Castro had stolen. So, the U.S. cut off all trade with the island and began to look for a way to get rid of Castro.

President John Kennedy, who was elected in 1960, agreed to allow a group of American trained Cuban refugees to attack the island in 1961. They landed at the Bay of Pigs in April of 1961. Kennedy refused, however, to give the invasion any real military help. As a result of that and poor planning, the

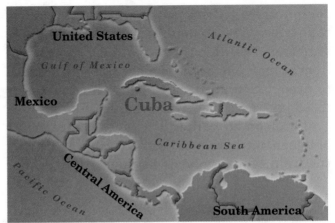

invasion failed, the refugees were killed or imprisoned and America looked really stupid.

A much more serious crisis occurred in 1962, the Cuban Missile Crisis. In fact, this was one of the most serious crises in the whole Cold War. It began in October when America learned that the Soviet Union was building missile bases in Cuba. If the Soviet Union put missiles there, they would be able to attack the United States all along the east coast. America could not allow them to have that kind of power.

President Kennedy decided to blockade the island to stop the missiles from being delivered, which were coming by ship. He also demanded that the U.S.S.R. remove the bases. The U.S. navy surrounded Cuba and was prepared to stop the Soviet ships, which might have started a war. Instead, the Soviet Union agreed not to send the missiles and took the bases down.

Little Wars. All over the earth during the Cold War, the U.S. and the Soviet Union took sides in little wars. They usually followed the same pattern. A group of some kind would decide they wanted to overthrow the government of their country. They would get help from one of the two super powers to do it. Immediately, the other super power would help the government to stay in power. In this way, dozens of little wars all over the world became Cold War battles.

These wars became longer and more dangerous than they would have been because both sides could get money and good weapons. Unfortunately, the U.S. believed it had no choice if it wanted to stop communism from spreading to more countries. The communists were constantly starting what they called "wars of liberation." These were wars to force nations to accept communism. Calling them wars for freedom was another communist lie.

It seemed like every disagreement between nations and every civil war during the Cold War involved the super powers. For example, the U.S. supported Israel in several wars after it was established in 1948. The Soviet Union supported its Arab enemies. Ethiopia, Angola, Nicaragua, Peru, El Salvador, and Afghanistan all had civil wars with opposite sides supported by the U.S. and U.S.S.R. The two super powers did not fight each other, but many people still died in the Cold War.

IMAGES FROM THE ARAB-ISRAELI WARS

 Give the information requested.

2.12   The year Joseph Stalin died _____

2.13   The leader of the Soviet Union that wanted peaceful coexistence

_____

2.14   The name used when the Cold War got a little warmer and the super powers nicer

_____

2.15   Type of spy plane shot down over the U.S.S.R. in 1960 _____

2.16   What happened in many little wars all over the world during the Cold War

_____

_____

2.17   a. What the Cuban Missile Crisis was about

_____

_____

_____

b. How President Kennedy acted to stop the Soviets in the Cuban Missile Crisis

_____

_____

c. How the Crisis ended _____

_____

2.18 Communist dictator of Cuba _____

2.19 American spy pilot shot down over the U.S.S.R. in 1960

_____

2.20 Place where U.S. trained Cuban refugees tried to invade Cuba in 1961

_____

2.21 What a communist "war of liberation" was

_____

_____

2.22 What happened to Austria in 1955

_____

_____

Vietnam War

Background. The Vietnam War was the longest and most **controversial** war in American history. It lasted from 1957 until 1975. However, America fought mainly between 1965 and 1973.

Vietnam had been part of French Indochina before World War II. After the war the Vietnamese wanted independence. France refused and sent an army to retake the nation. The Vietnamese army was led by a communist named Ho Chi Mihn who was helped by China. His followers were called the Vietmihn. Because they were fighting communists, America helped the French, but the French army still lost in 1954. A peace treaty divided the nation at the 17th parallel. The north became communist and the south did not.

South Vietnam was not a free country, but it was not communist. The leader of South Vietnam refused to allow elections to reunite the country in 1955. He argued that the communists could not be trusted to take part in fair elections. The U.S. agreed and supported him.

America Helps. The ruler of South Vietnam, Ngo Dinh Diem, was cruel and unpopular. In 1957 the communists in South Vietnam, called the Viet Cong, rebelled. The Vietmihn sent them supplies and weapons that came from China and the U.S.S.R. This was the beginning of the war.

At first, America sent military men to teach the South Vietnamese how to organize and fight. They did not actually fight, but some were killed. The government and army in South Vietnam was so bad that thousands of these **advisers** had to be sent. At the same time, the Viet Cong were winning because Diem was so unpopular. Then, Diem

THE VIETNAM WAR

began to persecute the Buddhists in his country, which made matters even worse. Diem was finally killed by the army, which took over the government in 1963.

The new government could not control the people. Many South Vietnamese believed it was an American controlled government, not one that really wanted what was best for them. By 1964, the Viet Cong controlled most of South Vietnam.

Gulf of Tonkin. The U.S. had sent navy ships to attack North Vietnam. One of these ships was apparently attacked in the Gulf of Tonkin in 1964. Afraid that South Vietnam would fall to the communists, President Lyndon Johnson asked Congress to let him to do something about it. Using the attack on the U.S. Navy as an excuse, Congress passed the *Gulf of Tonkin Resolution*. This resolution gave the president a lot of power to do whatever was needed to stop the communists in Vietnam, however the U.S. never declared war. In early 1965, Johnson sent the first American troops into Vietnam to fight, not to give advice.

War Going Nowhere. By 1964, the North Vietnamese army was also fighting in South Vietnam. They kept fighting even when they were defeated time after time in battle. The Viet Cong and Vietmihn hid in the jungle, attacked in small groups, set traps for U.S. soldiers and tried not to get into large battles. The U.S. used its many weapons, helicopters, and planes to defeat the communists in South Vietnam whenever they could find them. The U.S. also bombed North Vietnam to try to stop it from sending supplies and men to the South.

However, none of the American victories mattered. After the Americans won battles the North Vietnamese just sent more men and weapons (given to them by China and the U.S.S.R.). The U.S. had over 500,000 soldiers in Vietnam in 1969. All those men still could not win the war.

The government of South Vietnam made matters much worse. It was corrupt and unpopular. Many people in the United States thought it was not worth having American men die to defend such a bad government. Finally, a new president, Richard Nixon, decided to get America out of the war.

When he became president in 1969, Nixon began a new plan for the war. He worked to teach the South Vietnamese how to do the fighting and get the Americans out of the war. He also began to negotiate with the North Vietnamese to end the war. To force them to negotiate he ordered more bombing and attacks.

Finally, in 1973 the North Vietnamese agreed to a cease fire. They also agreed to send home all the American soldiers held by the Viet Cong and Vietmihn. Many of these men had been held for years in horrible places and were tortured by the communists. The American soldiers were taken out of South Vietnam during the cease fire. However, nothing was done to protect South Vietnam. North Vietnam even kept its army in the South.

Soon after the Americans left, the war started again. This time there were no American soldiers to hold off the Vietmihn. They quickly began to defeat the southern army. The American Congress refused to send any more help. In April of 1975, North Vietnam captured the southern capital of Saigon and reunited the nation under a communist government. Saigon was renamed Ho Chi Mihn City and thousands of Vietnamese were killed or imprisoned by the new government. Thousands more risked their lives by leaving the county in small, leaky boats to reach freedom in some other land.

 Answer *true* **or** *false.*

2.23 _____ The U.S. won the war in Vietnam.

2.24 _____ Ngo Dinh Diem was a popular, good ruler in South Vietnam.

2.25 _____ Ho Chi Mihn was the leader of the Vietnamese communists.

2.26 _____ South Vietnam was communist while the North was free in 1957.

2.27 _____ The Gulf of Tonkin Resolution declared war on North Vietnam.

2.28 _____ The Viet Cong were the North Vietnamese communists.

2.29 _____ North Vietnam got its supplies from the Soviet Union and China.

2.30 _____ The French were able to retake Vietnam after World War II.

2.31 _____ Many of the American prisoners in Vietnam were treated very cruelly.

2.32 _____ North Vietnam won the war when it captured Saigon in 1975.

2.33 _____ The two sides agreed to a cease fire in 1973 which allowed the American soldiers to leave Vietnam.

2.34 _____ The U.S. army could defeat the Vietmihn in battles, but could not get them to give up.

2.35 _____ Vietnam became a free country in 1975.

Review the material in this section in preparation for the Self Test. The Self Test will check your mastery of this particular section and the previous section. The items missed on this Self Test will indicate specific areas where restudy is needed for mastery.

SELF TEST 2

Match these people (each answer, 2 points).

2.01	_____ President who decided not to allow aggression in Korea	a. Douglas MacArthur
2.02	_____ President who forced the Soviets not to deliver missiles to Cuba	b. Harry S. Truman
2.03	_____ Senator who made claims about communists in the government	c. Nikita Khrushchev
2.04	_____ American spy pilot shot down over the U.S.S.R.	d. Francis Gary Powers
2.05	_____ State Department employee who lied about being a communist spy	e. Fidel Castro
2.06	_____ Communist dictator of Cuba	f. John Kennedy
2.07	_____ Communist dictator of China	g. Ho Chi Mihn
2.08	_____ Communist leader in Vietnam	h. Mao Zedong
2.09	_____ U.N. commander in the Korean War	i. Joseph McCarthy
2.010	_____ Soviet leader who lied about wanting peaceful coexistence	j. Alger Hiss

Name the person, crisis, item, or place (each answer, 3 points).

2.011 _____ Part of Korea that was communist

2.012 _____ Line around Pusan held by the U.N. at the beginning of the Korean War

2.013 _____ U.S. policy toward communism all during the Cold War, started by Harry S. Truman

2.014 _____ Place where American trained Cuban refugees tried to invade the island in 1961 and failed

2.015 _____ A type of government that owns everything, allows no freedom, and lies constantly.

2.016 _____ U.S. program that gave money to Europe to rebuild after World War II

2.017 _____ Treaty organization to protect Europe from the Soviet Union

2.018 _____ Part of Vietnam that was communist when war began there

2.019 _____ Part of Vietnam that was communist when the war there ended

2.020 _____ Nation that sent "volunteers" to help the communists in Korea

Answer these questions (each answer, 4 points).

2.021 Why did Harry Truman fire the American general in command in the Korean War?

_____

_____

_____

2.022 What kept the communists from making peace for a long time in Korea?

_____

_____

2.023 What was a "thaw" in the Cold War? _____

_____

2.024 What was the Cuban Missile Crisis? _____

_____

_____

2.025 What happened in wars all over the world during the Cold War? _____

_____

_____

2.026 What was the Gulf of Tonkin Resolution? _____

_____

_____

2.027 Why didn't the U.S. battle victories in Vietnam force the communists to surrender?

_____

_____

_____

2.028 What was the Berlin Wall and why was it put up? _____

_____

_____

2.029   What was the Iron Curtain?

_____

_____

2.030   What happened to Hungary and Czechoslovakia when they tried to end or change
         communism in their countries during the Cold War?

_____

_____

Write *true* **or** *false* **in the blank.** (each answer, 2 points).

2.031   _____   Taiwan held the Chinese seat in the U.N. after the communists took
                       over China.

2.032   _____   Vietnam was the longest and most controversial war in American
                       history.

2.033   _____   America did not win the war in Vietnam.

2.034   _____   North and South Korea were reunited after the Korean War.

2.035   _____   Chiang Kai-shek was the Nationalist leader in China.

III. UPHEAVAL IN AMERICA

Post-war America was in **upheaval**, especially in the 1960s. African Americans, under the leadership of Martin Luther King, Jr., demanded equal rights with white Americans. Ever since they had been freed from slavery, African Americans had never been treated fairly or given the same rights as white people. They staged protests, marches, and gave public speeches to push for change. Change came, but at a price.

In the meantime, the young people of America also rose in protest. These were "baby boomers," a huge group of people born after World War II. They wanted to change all kinds of things about America, especially to end the Vietnam War. They protested in large, loud, and angry crowds for the changes they wanted. This section will discuss all this upheaval and how the government reacted.

Review these objectives. When you have completed this section, you should be able to:

2. Describe the events and crises of the Cold War.
5. Describe the Civil Rights Movement.
6. Describe the protests and rebellions of the 1960s.
7. Name the presidents and describe their activities from 1945 to 1973.

Restudy these words.

character	idealist	immoral
rebellious	upheaval	

Civil Rights

Background. *Civil rights* is a name for the rights we have as citizens. The Civil Rights Movement is a name for the effort by African Americans to receive equal and fair treatment in the United States. This movement began in 1955.

After the Civil War gave black slaves their freedom, all kinds of laws were passed in the south to make sure they were not equal with whites. "Jim Crow" laws required that blacks and whites had separate facilities, like parks, public bathrooms, drinking fountains, and schools. The ones for whites were always better than those set aside for black people. Laws like poll taxes (a tax to vote), literacy tests (you had to read to vote, blacks almost always flunked the unfair test), and grandfather clauses (you could not vote unless your ancestors had voted in 1860) kept black people from voting. Any black man who did try to change things

was often beaten up or killed, and the white police would not arrest people who did it. Thus, freedom was not very free for African Americans.

School Desegregation. Schools in the south were *segregated* in the 1950s. That meant the white children went to one school and the black children to another. This was legal because of a decision by the Supreme Court in 1896 called *Plessy v. Ferguson.* The Court said that "separate but equal" facilities (like schools) for white and black people were fine. However, the facilities were never equal. White schools were often new with good textbooks and plenty of supplies. Black students would go to school in old, leaky buildings, use worn-out textbooks that weren't good enough for white students, and often had few supplies like chalk, paper, and desks. In the 1950s, another case reached the Supreme Court on the same issue.

"Free at last! free at last! thank God Almighty, we are free at last!"

THE CIVIL RIGHTS MOVEMENT. CLOCKWISE FROM TOP LEFT: ROSA PARKS ON THE BUS—BEING ARRESTED—IN THE MID-1990S, MARTIN LUTHER KING, KING IN A MARCH, GUARDS ESCORTING BLACK STUDENTS TO SCHOOL.

This time, in 1954, the Supreme Court changed its mind. In the decision *Brown v. the Board of Education of Topeka*, the Court ruled that separate schools were always unequal just by the fact they were separate. It was not fair to send children to separate schools just because of their skin color. The Court ordered that all southern schools had to be desegregated. They had to admit both white and black students.

Many white people in the south did not want black people to have equal rights. It was very hard to desegregate the schools in the south. In 1957, following a court order, Central High School in Little Rock, Arkansas tried to admit nine African American students. Mobs gathered outside the school and the governor brought in the national guard to stop the black students.

President Eisenhower, however, was not going to stand for that! He ordered the army to Little Rock to escort the students to class. Every day, the nine black teenagers would be picked up by army cars and taken to school. A group of soldiers, with guns, would surround them and march them into school. They often had to pass through a mob of angry people yelling and cursing at them. Inside the school, a soldier would stay with each student to make sure they were not hurt. It was an awful experience for those nine young people. However, those brave students began the change that finally gave African Americans the right to go to any school in the United States.

Montgomery Bus Boycott. Most historians say that the Civil Rights Movement began in 1955 with the *Montgomery Bus Boycott*. The buses in Montgomery, Alabama were segregated. Black people were supposed to sit in the back of the bus and leave the front seats for white people. One day in 1955, a black woman named Rosa Parks sat in the front of the bus and refused to move. She was arrested. The black people of Alabama decided to do something to stop this.

A local pastor named Rev. Martin Luther King, Jr. led the community in organizing to fight the bus segregation. He led a peaceful bus boycott. For months, black people refused to ride the buses. The bus companies lost money and the boycott attracted attention all over the nation. Finally, the courts agreed that segregation was illegal and the buses were desegregated. That victory was the beginning of the work of Martin Luther King for full and equal rights for African Americans.

Peaceful Protest. King's method was peaceful protest. He and his people were determined not to fight. They would simply and peacefully do what they were not allowed to do by the Jim Crow laws. They would, for example, go into restaurants that did not serve black people. They would sit down and refuse to move until they were served. Often they were arrested and sometimes beaten up. However, they never fought back or did anything violent in return. The courts began to side with them, ordering the states to stop segregation. Also, the press wrote about all of this and showed it on TV. Many Americans realized that blacks were being treated unfairly and began to support the Civil Rights Movement.

King also organized marches to protest segregation and laws that kept black people from voting. When he and his supporters tried to march peacefully through Birmingham, Alabama in 1963 they were attacked by the police. The unarmed people were knocked against the walls by water from fire hoses, attacked by police dogs, and shocked with cattle prods. The whole thing was seen on national television and caused an outcry of support for King and his marchers.

In August of that same year, King led his most famous march, the March on Washington. Thousands of people marched to the Lincoln Memorial to show their support for a new Civil Rights Act to protect the rights of African Americans. There, Martin Luther King gave his most famous speech called "I Have a Dream." It was all about how he dreamed of a nation of freedom and equality. He dreamed of having his children judged by their **character**, not their skin color. He dreamed of real freedom for all Americans, including black people.

The Civil Rights Movement almost created a war in the south. Crowds of black people who protested were often attacked by crowds of angry white people. The first black man to attend the University of Mississippi had to have an army escort. Civil rights workers were often shot down in cold blood. The nation was torn between those wanting to make things right and those who refused to consider it.

The Civil Rights Act was finally passed in 1964. It forbade any kind of segregation in public and protected the rights of black people to vote. The Voting Rights Act of 1965 ended literacy tests and put the federal government in charge of registering voters in several southern states. Court decisions all over the south also forced segregation to end and gave black people a chance to enjoy the rights of American citizens. Rev. King continued to preach and work for equality until he was assassinated in 1968.

It took years of protests, court decisions, arrests, and violence, but the Civil Rights Movement was a huge success. It forced America to live up to its own claim to be the "land of the free." As a result of the work of Martin Luther King and those who dared to protest with him, African Americans were finally given full and equal legal rights in the United States.

Complete these sentences.

3.1 The leader of the Civil Rights Movement was _____
_____ .

3.2 The way Rev. Martin Luther King worked was using _____
protests.

3.3 The event that started the Civil Rights Movement was the
_____ in 1955.

3.4 Martin Luther King's most famous speech was _____
_____ which he gave at the Lincoln Memorial during the
March on _____ in 1963.

3.5 _____ Laws in the south required separate facilities for
white and black people.

3.6 The _____ Act of 1964 forbade segregation and the
_____ Act of 1965 ended literacy tests for voting.

3.7 The Supreme Court decision that allowed segregation in 1896, _____
_____ , was changed by another decision,
_____ , that forbade it in
1954.

3.8 The first nine Blacks students to attend Central High School in Little Rock, Arkansas
got in only with an escort of _____ .

3.9 The woman who started the Montgomery Bus Boycott by refusing to move to the back
of the bus was _____ .

3.10 Martin Luther King Jr. was assassinated in _____ .

Protests and Politics

Protests. Because the Civil Rights Movement worked, many people tried protesting to change other things. Thousands of babies had been born after World War II. These "baby boomers" became restless teenagers in the 1960s. They led protests all over the nation on many subjects. They protested mainly at universities, where large groups of young adults lived. They protested for changes in college classes, for women's rights, against pollution, against poverty, and in favor of illegal drugs.

These young adults also rebelled against all of the rules they could find. They began to use illegal drugs and try out all kinds of **immoral** things. They wanted loud music and wild art. They disliked marriage and families. As a result of the changes they brought to America, we have high rates of divorce, abortion, and drug problems today.

Some of these people became known as "Hippies." Hippies rebelled against everything. They grew their hair long, seldom worked, used drugs, were often homeless, and claimed to be at peace with the world. They wandered around the country in groups or gathered on farms where they worked together to raise food to eat, sharing everything. In time, however, most of them realized they could not live like that forever. They got jobs and became a part of regular American life.

The protesters and hippies of the 1960s were **idealists**. They believed that they could change the world and fix all of its problems. They did not believe that the world's biggest problem was sin. They thought it was poverty, pollution, lack of education, or bad leaders. They tried to solve the wrong problems, in the wrong way, by themselves, without God.

Anti-war. The most wide-spread protests of the 1960s and early '70s were the anti-war protests. The rebels hated the Vietnam War. It was very unpopular, especially among the young men who were being drafted into the army. It is difficult to describe just how much the Vietnam War was hated in America.

There were many reasons why Americans hated the war. The cost of the war was tremendous in both money and lives. Many people felt we had no business fighting to keep the awful South Vietnamese government in power. The U.S. government kept saying that America was winning the war, but year after year the communists kept fighting. People began to believe the government was lying to them.

Protests against the war in Vietnam began in 1965, mainly at universities. Thousands of people would join the protests, which spread all over the country. Sometimes they would fight with the police. Some **rebellious** young men refused to register for the draft. Some fled to Canada rather than

ANTI-WAR PROTESTERS

serve in the army when they were drafted. In 1969, over 200,000 people marched on Washington to protest against the war. In 1970, four people were killed when soldiers shot at the students protesting at Kent State University. It seemed like the whole nation was fighting someone or something about the war.

Court Actions. The Supreme Court was also changing things in ways that upset much of the nation. The Warren Court, the Supreme Court led by Chief Justice Earl Warren, made many unpopular decisions in the 1950s and '60s. This was the court that ended segregation and protected civil rights. It also required that people accused of crimes had to be provided with a free lawyer if they needed it and have their constitutional rights protected. This Court also banned school prayer. Thus, even the Court was changing the nation and adding to the confusion in the country.

35

PRESIDENT JOHN F. KENNEDY

PRESIDENT LYNDON B. JOHNSON

PRESIDENT RICHARD M. NIXON

Politics. Dwight Eisenhower was a World War II hero and a popular president from 1953 to 1961. He did not push civil rights and really did not try to make any major changes in America. The one thing he did start in America was the huge system of highways that now runs all over our nation. However, the president who followed Eisenhower, John F. Kennedy, was much more interested in change. Kennedy was a young president, he was only 43 when he took office, and he wanted changes.

Kennedy called his program the New Frontier. He wanted to spend government money to make things better in America. He wanted civil rights, help for schools, and help for the poor. He wanted Americans to get involved and change the world. He started the Peace Corp which sent thousands of volunteers all over the world to help people in poorer countries. He had many of the ideals of the protesters.

However, the 1960s were also a time of violence. In 1963, President Kennedy was assassinated. A man named Lee Harvey Oswald shot the president with a rifle while Kennedy was riding in an open car in Dallas, Texas. Two days later someone else killed Oswald when he was being moved at the police station.

Kennedy was not the only leader assassinated in the 60s. Martin Luther King was shot by James Earl Ray, who was sent to prison for life. When King was killed in 1968, black people all over the nation rioted destroying property and hurting people. John Kennedy's brother, Robert Kennedy, was also assassinated. He was killed in 1968 while campaigning to become the Democratic candidate for president. The assassinations, riots and protests horrified the nation. Many did not believe America could survive all of this.

When John Kennedy was assassinated, his vice president, Lyndon Johnson, became president. Johnson was able to use his own skills and the sympathy over Kennedy's death to get many of the young president's ideas through Congress (which had not passed them before that). Johnson saw passage of the Civil Rights Act of 1964 and the Voting Rights Act. He was elected president in 1964.

His program was called the Great Society and it was supposed to end poverty in America. However, in 1965, he began sending soldiers to fight in Vietnam using the Gulf of Tonkin Resolution. The huge cost of the war in Vietnam made it impossible to pay for the Great Society. As the war became more and more unpopular, so did Johnson. He realized he would have trouble if he ran for president in 1968, so he decided not to run.

The Democratic Party met in Chicago to choose a candidate. Robert Kennedy, who was the most popular anti-war candidate, had been assassinated. Anti-war protesters fought with the police anywhere the Democrats were meeting. It was all shown on television, too. The Democrats chose vice president Hubert Humphery who was in favor of the war. He lost the election to Republican Richard Nixon, who had been Dwight Eisenhower's vice president.

Nixon worked to end the war. He tried to force the North Vietnamese to sign a peace treaty by bombing and attacking hard. That increased the anti-war protests in America. However, Nixon was only able to get a cease fire by 1973. He used the break in the fighting to get the American soldiers out of Vietnam. With the war over, as far as Americans were concerned, the protests quickly died. Within two years, South Vietnam surrendered, and Vietnam became a communist nation.

Vietnam was the only war in our history in which the U.S. failed. We were not able to defeat the Vietnamese communists. This hurt America deeply. Some people believed that we could have won if we had just supported the army. Those people blamed the protesters for taking away that support. Other people believed that we were wrong to get so deeply into a nasty civil war in a foreign land. They blamed our leaders for making bad decisions. Other people came to distrust the government so much they believed that our leaders even lied about why we got into the war in the first place. Thus, America was, and still is, very divided about what was right or wrong in the Vietnam War. Americans have trusted their government less since Vietnam.

Answer these questions.

3.11   What were the most wide-spread protests of the 1960s and '70s about?

_____

3.12   Who were the four presidents between 1953 and 1970?

_____

_____

3.13   Who are the "Baby Boomers?" _____

_____

3.14   What bad changes have come to America because of the rebellion of the 1960s?

_____

_____

3.15   How did some rebellious young men in the 1960s react to the draft?

_____

_____

3.16   Who was the Supreme Court Justice whose court approved civil rights, but also

ended prayer in schools? _____

3.17 Who assassinated John F. Kennedy? _____

Martin Luther King, Jr.? _____

3.18 Who were Hippies? _____

_____

3.19 What happened outside the Democratic Party meeting in Chicago in 1968?

_____

_____

3.20 How did Nixon get the American soldiers out of Vietnam?

_____

_____

3.21 What was Lyndon Johnson's program and why was there not enough money for it?

_____

3.22 What was John Kennedy's program and when was it passed by Congress?

_____

_____

3.23 What is the Peace Corp and who started it?

_____

_____

3.24 Who first sent soldiers to fight in Vietnam under the Gulf of Tonkin Resolution?

_____

3.25 Why did the Vietnam War hurt America so much?

_____

_____

Before you take this last Self Test, you may want to do one or more of these self checks.

1. _____ Read the objectives. Determine if you can do them.
2. _____ Restudy the material related to any objectives that you cannot do.
3. _____ Use the SQ3R study procedure to review the material:
   a. **S**can the sections.
   b. **Q**uestion yourself again (review the questions you wrote initially).
   c **R**ead to answer your questions.
   d **R**ecite the answers to yourself.
   e **R**eview areas you didn't understand.
4. _____ Review all activities and Self Tests, writing a correct answer for each wrong answer.

SELF TEST 3

Match these people (each answer, 2 points).

3.01 _____ President who got U.S. soldiers out of Vietnam

    a. John Kennedy

3.02 _____ Assassinated John Kennedy

    b. Lyndon Johnson

3.03 _____ Young president, started the Peace Corp, New Frontier

    c. Martin Luther King

3.04 _____ Chief Justice, Supreme Court; banned school prayer, helped civil rights

    d. Earl Warren

    e. Rosa Parks

3.05 _____ Assassinated Martin Luther King, Jr.

    f. Richard Nixon

3.06 _____ War hero president who started the highway system

    g. Dwight Eisenhower

3.07 _____ The Civil Rights Movement began when she refused to move to the back of the bus

    h. Douglas MacArthur

    i. Lee Harvey Oswald

3.08 _____ U.N. commander in the Korean War

    j. James Earl Ray

3.09 _____ Leader of the Civil Rights Movement, used peaceful protest

3.010 _____ U.S. president who first sent soldiers to Vietnam under the Gulf of Tonkin Resolution

Name the person, event, place, or thing (each answer, 3 points).

3.011 _____ Laws in the south that set up segregation of blacks

3.012 _____ The most wide-spread protests of the 1960s and 70s were about this

3.013 _____ Large group of people born right after World War II

3.014 _____ Cold War Crisis in which Cuba was blockaded to stop the delivery of missiles

3.015 _____ Dividing line between the free countries and communist countries in Cold War Europe

3.016 _____ Treaty organization to protect Europe during the Cold War, the U.S. joined

3.017 _____ Leader of the communists in China during the civil war there

3.018 _____ Martin Luther King's most famous speech

3.019 _____ First man-made satellite, launched in 1957

3.020 _____ Island that the U.S. said was the government of China after the communists took over China

Answer these questions (each answer, 4 points).

3.021 What was "separate but equal" really like in the south?

_____

_____

_____

3.022 How did nine black students first go to Central High School in Little Rock, Arkansas? _____

_____

3.023 How did civil rights workers fight segregation laws?

_____

_____

3.024 What did the rebellions of the 1960s cause in America?

_____

_____

3.025 How did some rebellious young men react to the draft in the 1960s?

_____

_____

3.026 Why was the Vietnam War so hard on Americans?

_____

_____

3.027 What is communism?

_____

_____

3.028 What did the Civil Rights Movement change?

_____

_____

3.029   What was the Berlin Wall?

_____

_____

3.030   What was the U.S. policy of Containment during the Cold War?

_____

_____

Write _true_ **or** _false_ **in the blank** (each answer, 2 points).

3.031   _____ The court decision _Plessy v. Ferguson_ in 1896 made segregation illegal in American schools.

3.032   _____ Hippies rebelled against everything.

3.033   _____ Anti-war protesters fought with the police at the 1968 Democratic Party meeting in Chicago.

3.034   _____ The Korean War was the longest and most controversial war in American history.

3.035   _____ Goods like shoes and cars are usually very well made in communist countries.

80
100

Score
Adult Check _____

           Initial   **Date**

Before you take the LIFEPAC Test, you may want to do one or more of these self checks.

1. _____ Read the objectives. Determine if you can do them.

2. _____ Restudy the material related to any objectives that you cannot do.

3. _____ Use the SQ3R study procedure to review the material:

4. _____ Review all activities and Self Tests, and LIFEPAC Glossary.

5. _____ Restudy areas of weakness indicated by the last Self Test.